be still

ILLUSTRATED BY

SARAH CRAY

Gibbs Smith

TO ENRICH & INSPIRE HUMANKIND

QUIET THE MIND

AND THE SOUL

WILL SPEAK

MINDFULNESS IS SIMPLY BEING AWARE OF WHAT IS HAPPENING RIGHT NOW WITHOUT WISHING IT WERE DIFFERENT: ENJOYING THE PLEASANT WITHOUT HOLDING ON WHEN IT CHANGES (WHICH IT WILL). BEING WITH THE UNPLEASANT WITHOUT FEARING IT WILL ALWAYS BE THIS WAY (WHICH IT WON'T).

James Baraz

Peace is the result of retraining your mind to process life as it is, rather than as you think it should be.

WAYNE W. DYER

If you feel lost, disappointed, hesitant, or weak, return to yourself, to who you are, here and now and when you get there, you will discover yourself, like a lotus flower in full bloom, even in a muddy pond, beautiful and strong.

MASARU EMOTO, *SECRET LIFE OF WATER*

There are only two ways to live your life. One is as though nothing is a miracle. The other is as though everything

is a miracle.

ALBERT EINSTEIN

AT TIMES,
PRODUCTIVITY
MEANS DOING
NOTHING AT ALL.

GINA GREENLEE,

Postcards and Pearls

When you do things from your Soul, you feel a river moving in you, a joy.

RUMI

ALWAYS HOLD FAST TO THE
PRESENT. EVERY SITUATION—
INDEED EVERY MOMENT—IS OF
INFINITE VALUE
FOR IT IS THE REPRESENTATIVE
OF A WHOLE ETERNITY.

Johann Wolfgang von Goethe

NEVER BE IN A HURRY: DO
EVERYTHING QUIETLY AND
IN A CALM SPIRIT.
DO NOT LOSE YOUR INNER
PEACE FOR ANYTHING
WHATSOEVER,
EVEN IF YOUR WHOLE
WORLD SEEMS UPSET.

St. Francis de Sales

EVERYTHING THAT HAS

A BEGINNING HAS AN

ENDING. MAKE YOUR

PEACE WITH THAT AND

ALL WILL BE WELL.

Jack Kornfield, BUDDHA'S LITTLE INSTRUCTION BOOK

In today's rush, we all think too much —seek too much — want too much and forget about the joy of just being.

ECKHART TOLLE

Choosing stillness in the midst of chaos is the path toward living in peace.

DEEPAK CHOPRA

The body benefits from movement,
and the mind benefits from
stillness.

SAKYONG MIPHAM,
RUNNING WITH THE MIND OF MEDITATION

WHAT YOU
FEED YOUR MIND,
LEADS YOUR LIFE.

Kemi Sogunle

BEGIN AT ONCE TO LIVE, AND COUNT EACH SEPARATE DAY AS A SEPARATE LIFE.

Seneca,
MORAL LETTERS TO LUCILIUS

If you cannot find peace within yourself, you will never find it anywhere else.

MARVIN GAYE

Peace is liberty in tranquility.

MARCUS TULLIUS CICERO

Worrying does not take away tomorrow's troubles, it takes away today's peace.

INSTEAD OF WORRYING
ABOUT WHAT YOU
CANNOT CONTROL,
SHIFT YOUR ENERGY
TO WHAT YOU CAN
CREATE

Roy T. Bennett

The present moment is the only time over which we have dominion.

THICH NHAT HANH, *THE MIRACLE OF MINDFULNESS*

WHATEVER THE PRESENT
MOMENT CONTAINS,
ACCEPT IT AS IF YOU
HAD CHOSEN IT. ALWAYS
WORK WITH IT, NOT
AGAINST IT.

Eckhart Tolle

To see a World in a grain of sand

And Heaven in a Wild Flower

Hold Infinity

in the palm of your hand,

And Eternity in an hour.

WILLIAM BLAKE,
"AUGURIES OF INNOCENCE"

Who looks outside,

dreams: who looks inside, awakes.

CARL JUNG

YOU ARE THE SKY, EVERYTHING ELSE—
IT'S JUST THE WEATHER.

Pema Chödrön

There are a thousand reasons to live this life, every one of them sufficient.

MARILYNNE ROBINSON, *GILEAD*

AS YOU WALK AND EAT
AND TRAVEL,
BE WHERE YOU ARE,
OTHERWISE YOU WILL
MISS MOST OF
YOUR LIFE.

JACK KORNFIELD,
Buddha's Little Instruction Book

That's life:

starting over,

one breath at a time.

SHARON SALZBERG, *REAL HAPPINESS*

I wish that life should not be cheap but sacred.

I wish the days to be as centuries, loaded, fragrant.

RALPH WALDO EMERSON,
THE CONDUCT OF LIFE

The ideal of calm exists in a sitting cat.

JULES RENARD

If the doors of perception were cleansed,

everything would appear to man as it is, infinite.

WILLIAM BLAKE

ONLY IN STILLNESS
DOES THE
IMPERCEIVABLE BECOME
DISCERNIBLE.

BRYANT MCGILL, *Simple Reminders*

A few simple tips for life:

feet on the ground,

head to the skies,

heart open...quiet mind.

RASHEED OGUNLARU

"forever is composed of nows"

EMILY DICKINSON

BE HAPPY IN
THAT'S
EACH MOMENT

THE MOMENT,
ENOUGH.

IS ALL WE NEED.

Mother Teresa

Compassion is not complete if it does not include oneself.

ALLAN LOKOS,
PATIENCE: THE ART OF PEACEFUL LIVING

True happiness is to enjoy the present, without anxious dependence upon the future.

LUCIUS ANNAEUS SENECA

If you want to conquer the anxiety of life, live in the moment, live in the breath.

AMIT RAY,
OM CHANTING AND MEDITATION

To be sensual, I think, is to respect and rejoice in the force of life, of life itself, and to be present in all that one does, from the effort of loving to the breaking of bread.

JAMES BALDWIN,
THE FIRE NEXT TIME

The present moment is filled
with joy and happiness.
If you are attentive,
you will see it.

THICH NHAT HANH

*Perfection of character is this:
to live each day as if
it were your last, without
frenzy, without apathy,
without pretense.*

MARCUS AURELIUS,
MEDITATIONS

The privilege of a lifetime is to become who you truly are.

CARL JUNG

In this moment,

there is plenty of time.

In this moment you are

precisely as you should be.

In this moment,

there is infinite possibility.

VICTORIA MORAN, *YOUNGER BY THE DAY*

Life is
a collection
of moments.

Mindfulness is beautification of the moments.

AMIT RAY,
MINDFULNESS

Within you there is a stillness and a sanctuary to which you can retreat at any time and be yourself.

HERMANN HESSE, *SIDDARTHA*

The hour through which you are at meet here and now, the task on moment —these are always the most present passing, the man whom you which you are enjoyed at this very important in your whole life.

PAUL EVDOKIMOV

WHEN YOU
REALIZE NOTHING
IS LACKING,
THE WHOLE WORLD
BELONGS TO YOU.

Lao Tzu

The grass is not 'greener'
on the other side —
it is just another
shade of green.

ANNIKA SORENSON,
TAKE STRESS FROM CHAOS TO CALM

Authenticity is the daily practice of letting go of who we think we're supposed to be and embracing who we are.

BRENÉ BROWN,
THE GIFTS OF IMPERFECTION

The most precious gift we can offer others is our presence. When our mindfulness embraces those we love, they will bloom like flowers.

THICH NHAT HANH

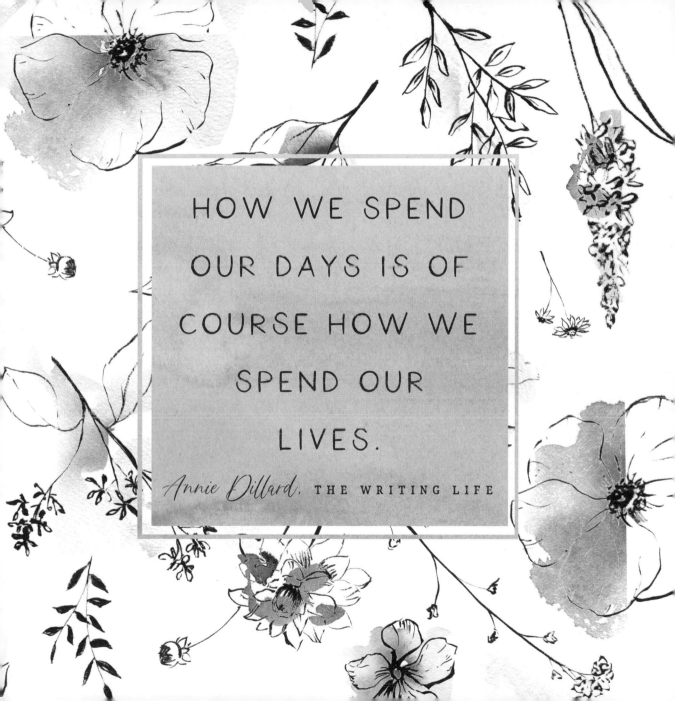

HOW WE SPEND
OUR DAYS IS OF
COURSE HOW WE
SPEND OUR
LIVES.

Annie Dillard, THE WRITING LIFE

Be still,
Stillness reveals the
secrets of eternity.

LAO TZU

SARAH CRAY
IS THE CREATOR OF DANDELION
PAPER CO. AND "LET'S MAKE ART," AN
ONLINE COMMUNITY AND ART SUPPLY SHOP,
WITH THE GOAL OF GETTING MORE PEOPLE TO
PAINT AND TO LIVE A MORE CREATIVE LIFE. HER
PREVIOUS BOOKS, *MOTHERHOOD* AND *SISTERHOOD*,
PAY HOMAGE TO OUR MOST VALUABLE FEMALE
BONDS. SARAH LIVES IN HAMILTON,
MISSOURI, WITH HER FAMILY.

TO MICHAEL, BECAUSE HE IS
MY HEART AND MY PEACE.

First Edition

24 23   5 4

Text © 2020 Gibbs Smith Publisher

Illustrations © 2020 Sarah Cray

Published by
Gibbs Smith
P.O. Box 667
Layton, Utah 84041

1.800.835.4993 orders

www.gibbs-smith.com

Printed and bound in China

Gibbs Smith books are printed on either recycled, 100% post-
consumer waste, FSC-certified papers or on paper produced from
sustainable PEFC-certified forest/controlled wood source. Learn
more at www.pefc.org.

Library of Congress Control Number:2019955364

ISBN: 978-1-4236-5446-9